CASTE: THE UNEXPLORED TERRITORIES

ROY T JAMES

PREFACE

This book is an attempt to present caste in its entirety, especially with reference to India, in a common relationship with life as is its starting point. For the reason that caste is an integral part of life. And, if you dissect life to examine it, what you end up examining is not life.

This book is also an attempt to offer a primer, providing essential information about caste from as many viewpoints as possible. For the reason that most of the books see caste as a collection of impositions having no regard to its life and, others see it as an abstraction summarizing one's persona, disregarding the pinpricks and hazards of its exterior. These two endeavors are not clearly delineated, as caste in reality exists everywhere as an inseparable union of both, in varying ratios and combinations. A peep inside shall then give the true picture, enhancing the pleasure of seeing one's interest in a richness of colors.

My motivation for writing this book came from three quarters.

I happened to get admitted to a military hospital for more than a year at a stretch with books as the only companions, the hospital being located far from the nearest urban dwelling. From the few books readily available for reading, I found 'Mahatma Gandhi-The Complete Works' deeply enjoyable and captivating. I also could discover in the author a very intelligent, discerning and practical individual, quite contrary to the image I had been maintaining all the while. It dawned on me that Mahatma Gandhi is being constantly hijacked by all, followers, opponents and congressmen alike, presenting him as someone deeply lovable or impractical or both, to keep his real self away from the public. I found in him, the only voice during the freedom struggle which advised those of lower caste to surpass the ones of upper caste by freely competing with them. He was also vehemently opposed to reservations of any kind, as it effectively nullified such a contest.

'The Complete Works' changed my very idea of caste, rooted in the exhortations, writings and discussions, I was constantly made to witness as part of the much celebrated 'Indian democracy'. These new findings further encouraged me to conduct my own research. And thanks to the little foray I made into the story of transition of Indian society, I now feel empowered to present a radically different view.

My efforts in reading 'The Complete Works' also brought to fore another occurrence of my younger days, an event connected with my school life, the unease caused by which has been lying dormant with me all these years. While in school, I witnessed the funeral of one of my teachers who happened to meet with an untimely death. And the deceased being from a highly influential and wealthy family of that locality, the observance of the ceremonies and events of his last rites was drawing quite a large crowd. When the body was about to be carried to the pyre, out from the crowd came a weak voice "Wait, I didn't get my share". The body was abruptly kept down by all those who have been positioned around for the ritual; the chanting of mantras came to an immediate stop along with all other accompaniments as though on a command. The ceremonies did resume only after paying that lowly servant his due. (According to his caste status, that consisted of a small towel and a tiny packet of rice!) I was stunned by the huge power, the weak voice could wield.

These memories brought with them still earlier days of my primary classes, when I, with a couple of my classmates used to walk to school every day, most of the times taking the path through an orchard. As we enter the orchard, one boy of our group (the smartest of us, I used to think!) would pluck a few fruits by stealth, which used to be shared by all of us making our school journey really interesting. One day when that boy was ill, I attempted to pluck some of them myself and was readily caught by the owner, though I had unfailingly followed my friend's evading tactics and style. He admonished me severely, however, offered a real handful of good fruits and advised: "If you want, you must ask, do not try to imitate what your friends do every day because they are of such and such caste, it is their rightful job". I could not fathom the rationale, that forced one to look elsewhere permitting one boy to steal some fruits and required the same one to stop looking elsewhere to prevent another boy from stealing any fruits.

Chapter 1

CASTE – A Look-over

As Shri Bhimrao Ambedkar says through his well-known essay "Caste in India, Genesis, Mechanism, and Development" (Indian Antiquary May 1917), "Subtler minds and abler pens than mine have been brought to the task of unraveling the mysteries of caste; but unfortunately it still remains in the domain of the 'unexplained' not to say of the 'unundersstood'" Never has this observation been more appropriate than now, when no aspect of social and political life of India is free of its influence. And this influence seems to be on the rise, notwithstanding the best efforts to the contrary by every right-thinking entity as well as the state. To unravel some of the mysteries this institution holds within, let us take a journey through its origin and development.

The definition of caste which has the approval of most sociologists is that caste is merely a rigid social class into which members are born and from which they can escape or withdraw with extreme difficulty. In other words, it is a type of stratification system, which is most rigid in matters of mobility and distinction of status. Caste, being the distinctive essence of India that attracted the visitors the most, has been studied at length and much has been written about its nature, especially the various rules, conventions and patterns that are meant for influencing and controlling its members. Surprisingly, a lot needs to be explained about the genesis of this social edifice, as its origins do not seem to have received enough attention. Some of the theories proposed are,

Racial theory - that caste system is a gift of Aryans,

Political theory - that caste system is an invention of Brahmins,

Occupational theory - that caste system is the functional differentiation of occupational differences,

Traditional theory - that caste system is of divine origin aimed to maintain social harmony,

Guild theory - that caste system is a natural product of interaction between guilds, tribes, and religion,

Religious theory - that caste system is nothing but the institutionalization of prevailing customs, each caste being the followers of certain deity, and,

Evolution theory - that caste system is a spin-off from the evolution of human society moderated by various factors, like prejudices, lack of control mechanisms, geographic isolation of Indian peninsula as well as conquerors' policies, especially that of the British, to name a few.

Chapter 2

THEORIES OF CASTE – A PEEP

2.1 Racial Theory: The fact that caste names Brahmana, Kshatriya, and Visya are frequently mentioned in the Rigveda along with words like 'dasa', 'varna', and many other words used these days in connection with caste, gives credence to the theory that caste is an invention of Indo-Aryans. In 'cultural history of India' AL Basham mentions that caste system evolved to accommodate a large variety of tribes into Aryan society during expansion of Vedic (ancient days) Aryan territories.

However, such delineation fails to notice the importance generally was ascribed to 'the moral worth' of a man rather than his 'birth' which, we can see at many places in ancient Indian literature.

The life of 'Eklavya' mentioned in 'Mahabharata' is one example. Eklavya was accepted by his teacher notwithstanding his low caste background, thanks to his sincerity and devotion. This clearly was against the norms that permitted only those of high caste to learn archery and fighting.

Also, such literature does not show much evidence indicating the practice of caste differentiation in daily life and demarcation of people on that basis.

In Al Baroonis India, he describes human, according to Indian thought, as consisting of twenty-five elements, soul (sattva, tamas, rajas), matter, nature, will etc, and one learning all these "will achieve salvation whatever religion one may follow".

Similar is the opinion of Sir Vincent Smith, who in 'Asoka-his History' says "Though each caste has its own dharma, the conduct is less rigid than it has been since Moslem invasions".

In short, almost every ancient book gives a different interpretation of caste, none of them pointing to a solid, definitive structure.

From all these, a conclusion one can reach is that caste, as we see now, needs a better explanation than that "it has been evolved during intermingling of Indo Aryan and local tribes".

2.2 Political Theory:

In Mahabharata (Shanti Parva) creation of caste is given thus: "Brahma created the world entirely Brahmanic. Later, those Brahmins fond of sensual pleasure became kshatriyas. Those Brahmins who subsisted by agriculture neglecting their duties entered the state of Vaisya and those who were fond of mischief and falsehood sank into the condition of Sudras".

In his study paper on 'Hindu Caste System and Hinduism', examining the dependence of vocations on heredity, Dr. Sharma explains the formation of caste thus: "To meet liturgical needs, the society from among themselves would select, on the basis of skills of elocution, the Brahmins. Similarly, for administrative purposes, those with qualities of leadership would be selected... Furthermore, *visha*(clan or tribe) also embodied people known as Shudra (meaning not of the tribe, newcomers) representing all newcomers to that particular tribe....Thus all responsibilities related to a *visha* could be grouped into four subcategories", each having "their duties and skills". (*www.geocities.com/lamberdar/_caste.html*)

Caste can thus be seen as having been a useful tool for maintaining social order, which though is a plausible definition, does not justify the more or less vicious form, it now maintains. This interpretation, by leaving out the conceptual element in the manifestation of caste identity, fails totally in putting forward an explanation for the rapid, natural growth of this social contraption and its wide acceptance.

2.3 Occupational theory: According to 'Theodosian' code, in early Roman Empire, a son was required to follow one's fathers' profession, thus maintaining the availability of skill while solving the question of the continuation of enterprises. That such an arrangement was widely followed can be observed in many of the popular surnames of today, Smith, Miller, Potter, to name a few.

Here, one question can come up. How these occupational guilds and other family groups metamorphosed into a rather solidified form, castes, in India, while they amalgamated fully into the larger social canvas in every other part of the world? Isn't it obvious that something India-specific was in action? More so, since almost all other institutions (other than the occupational guilds and other family groups) of the bygone era as far as India is concerned, together with all institutions of the same period as far as rest of the world goes, evolved naturally into something appropriate for the times.

2.4 Traditional theory, Guild theory, and Religious theory: These theories propose divine intervention in human affairs. Such intervention regulates society by maintaining harmony in all essential functions that are necessary for social well being, mankind being left free in search of bliss. Temporal groups could have originated randomly in the resulting social churning, and, quite understandably, they would have been following endogamy to continue their quest unhindered. You see, nobody would have liked to share such fruits of their labor with those not close enough. On the passage of time, these endogamous groups followed the natural path of converting themselves into a more permanent edifice - castes.

In this phenomenon of caste formation, some groups would find themselves becoming endogamous for certain benefits. Some others could find themselves forced into becoming so, by society, by closing all avenues of social interaction.

Such a theory, though may succeed in explaining the formation of castes as a singularity during the evolution of societies, fails in providing a valid reason for the continued existence of the vast expanse of castes and related observances, each more irrational than every other one, in Indian society.

2.5 Evolutionary theory: This hypothesis, in fact, is not an altogether new or different theory. It states, in effect, that over the years, the formation of caste did take place as a natural reaction to the influence exerted by all the factors we have seen earlier, in one form or other.

However, the most significant property of caste, the quality that differentiates it from all other social structures, is the resistance it shows to any change to its basic nature. Thus its capacity to differentiate between people of various groups, especially for the purpose of awarding social status, seems to have defied all natural forces of evolution that fell many an institution. This is but a strong indication that this is not a 'natural reaction to events'.

It is interesting to note that each one of the above theories is capable of explaining almost all the questions on the practice of caste system. The only area where the theories are found wanting is in the abstract nature of caste, and the ability to hold on to such a nature, notwithstanding its transition over the years.

It is quite likely that this facet of caste did not merit the attention of any of the early exponents. (Just like the present day enthusiasts, they also would have been totally blown out of the water by the outward show, caste continue to maintain) That is quite a possibility; because caste differences, being dormant or unobtrusive in a healthy society, would not have been resulting in inter-caste rivalries to bring such facets to fore. One has to remember, caste need not be visible at all, and it is the caste difference that protrudes.

This perhaps is what happened; all the theories missed the abstract, and its role in maintaining peace and harmony went unnoticed where harmony prevailed. And in disharmony, nothing of the abstract would have been of any help, to make its absence seen. As a result, all those who took interest in this subject were completely at home with whatever theory that caught their fancy.

Chapter 3

DEVELOPMENT OF CASTE - A GLIMPSE

3.1 The origin and development of caste system are closely linked to the evolution of Indian society, which, like any other society could have been having natural variation among its members. All we need is to narrow down our interest to the distinct features of this society, which could cause these abstract variations to transform into a more lasting, hardened form.

The stratification property of caste can be thought of as a carrier of such a transformation, since it can lead to changes that continue over generations. In fact, this is not a monopoly of India. Its mention can be found in many places, History by Herodotus as well as the description of Mande or Osu caste systems of Africa being examples. These, the division of people into four estates in medieval Europe, of feudal barons, clergy, urban merchants and the mass of people as well as, the grouping among old Israel population having ritual ramifications, are a few places where one can find established systems of differentiating humans to varying levels.

However, such a process of division has been a subject of study by sociologists. The eminent writer Herbert Spencer, in his sociological theories, have put forth following generalizations:

- The larger the number of people and internal transactions, greater will be the size and degree of internal differentiation of government.

- The greater the actual or potential level of conflict with other societies and unrest within a society, the more acute will be the degree of centralization of power in a government.

- The greater the centralization of power, the more visible class divisions will be and the more these divisions create actual or potential conflict.

Like colonies of all living species, dominant leadership and consequent concentration of power did happen in all cultures of the human race. Which have been giving rise to class structures of different flavor.

3.2 Thus we see, though the tendency to form social class is present in every society, and in the case of India, the stratification became increasingly stable, crystallizing into castes. The main factor which effected this transformation, of a flexible social class into a rigid caste, is another custom which slipped into Indian society, endogamy. Says Ambedker "Remember that endogamy is foreign to the people of India...It is no exaggeration to say that with the people of India exogamy is a creed and none dare infringe it...there are more rigorous penalties for violating exogamy than there are for violating endogamy. Castes, as far as India is concerned, means superposition of endogamy on exogamy".

His dissertation identifies that sati or enforced widowhood, where a widow is not allowed to remarry, the imposition of celibacy on widower as well as, girl marriage, came to be part of Indian "uxorial customs to maintain numerical parity between the two sexes". This in turn established endogamy in Indian society leading to the perpetuation of the caste system.

3.3 S Charles Hill says (Indian Antiquary March 1930) "Instead of allowing ourselves to be misled by the outward show of Hinduism we must concentrate our attention on what the Hindu writings tell us ... According to the Bhagavad Gita, to be truly wise, one must have learned:

- To control the body in its appetites and desires so that it does not injure itself or impede the free action of soul

- To act for benefit of the community without hope of reward... so long as one's duty as laid down by the requirement of caste is performed

- To resign oneself with absolute patience to pain and suffering and loss, and feel no exultation in success"

In other words, to fit oneself for the position of a ruler one must have overcome all human weaknesses and renounced all material rewards. In a similar vein is the discussion on matters related to requirements of other castes, and as such, the above is sufficient to show that what differentiates them is simply character. He continues, stressing the fact that more than one observer has commented on the "purity, regularity, equity, and strictness of the ancient Indian government". He further notes that the ideal Hindu kingdom is not a utopian dream, still exists in the hearts of Hindus, that it was based upon a social system which secured the happiness and contentment and loyalty of all classes of the people, and that the later stages of corruption and confusion have been due to foreign intrusion whether from central Asia or from Europe, whilst whatever unrest now prevails in India is caused by the incessant struggles of the Hindu caste ideal against alien influences. About the caste system existing then, he says, "... as a matter of fact, though we talk of upper and lower castes, no caste was originally considered superior or inferior...though in the Sudra the body is predominant, in the Vaisya the reason, in the Kshatriya the heart and in the Brahmin the soul, all castes are equally manifestations of Brahma though of different qualities. The relation between a higher and lower caste is then more like that between an adult and a child than that between a noble and a serf." He says further, "It provides every member of the community with a position which, though rigidly fixed, is fixed only by his natural limitations, and so allows him every opportunity of using to their full extent whatever abilities he may possess to the general advantage."

The views expressed by many exponents of ancient customs and traditions (http://www.palikanon.com/, Caste and Bhagawat Gita –OP Gupta, IFS) also are not dissimilar. Supporters of caste often quote two slokas viz. (IV.13) and (XVIII.41) of Shrimad Bhagwat Gita to support four castes by birth. Let us examine. In sloka (IV.13) Lord Krishna says: "Chaturvarnyma mayaa sristam gunkarma vibhagsah" i.e. four orders of society created by Me according to their Guna (qualities/behavior) and Karma (profession/work/efforts). Lord Krishna does not say guna and karma of previous life. In sloka (XVIII.41) Lord Krishna says "Brahmana Kshatriya visham sudranam cha paramtapa, karmani pravibhaktani svabhavaprabhavaigunaih." It means people have been grouped into four classes according to their present life karma (profession/work) and svabhava (behavior). `The division of labor into four categories - Brahman, Kshatriya, Vaishya, and Sudra - is also based on the Gunas inherent in peoples' nature`. Had this division be based on birth, Lord Krishna would have naturally used phrase 'Janani pravibhaktani' in the very shloka (XVIII.41). In sloka (XVIII.42), Lord Krishna prescribes duties (karma) which one must do in order to qualify as a Brahman i.e. among other duties (karma), he must have studied Vedas and must teach Vedas to others. Thus, "if a person has neither studied Veda nor teaches Veda to others, he is not a Brahman."

During the journeys of Hieun Tsang, he is said to have mentioned "... society consists of four caste groups. These four castes form classes for ceremonial purity." (as quoted at http://www.palikanon.com/)

Such a system, where social life is entirely independent of political government, naturally disintegrated when Indian society came into contact with various invading societies, the most potent intrusion being the one beginning with the landing of Portuguese adventurers at Calicut with VascoDaGama. All the invaders utilized the diversity in social positions among Indians as a convenience in governance, by according political legitimacy to existing differences. These variations, which were of academic interest (if at all) in life thus far, might have been of great use to the invading group in governing the land. It is probable that the visitors made use of such expedients in its differential form, an obvious choice for greater effect.

I think this would have effectively made caste status as something of immediate value in everyday life, rather than being the unchangeable shackles of the afterlife, which people have been conveniently and rather philosophically leaving to fate. It is also likely that people wanted to safeguard the thus legitimized privileges as close to oneself as possible. For enabling this, the populace might have chosen a quick, easy and very effective method – endogamy. The natural inclination among people of similar privileges to group together would have amply supported this.

3.4 Another view is expressed by Gail Omvedt, who in his book 'Caste race and sociologists' mentions that some writers, for example, Ronald Inden in his book 'Imagined India', puts forward an argument that caste can be seen as a product of 'western efforts to orientalize their conquered subjects'. Also, genomic studies pertaining to origins of castes conducted to identify differences in the distribution of genetic material among different caste groups points to such a conclusion.

In fact, many of those may point to similar inferences, that lineage of caste groups (nontribal population) show relationship with central Asia while most of the lineages of tribal groups are from original Indian gene pool. Thus, effectively, genes of upper caste population are from European stock, while those from lower caste population are from Asian stock. (see Molecular Anthropology' M Bamshad et al. http://jorde-lab.genetics.utah.edu/elibrary/Babshad_2001a.pdf)

But there are also many, who think otherwise. Partha Majumdar et al. (ISI Calcutta) reports after a comprehensive statistical analysis of data from ethnically diverse settlements of India, that, tribal and caste populations are highly differentiated and genetic histories have been considerably obliterated making it impossible to see any clear congruence of genetic affinities. (See 'Ethnic India- A Genomic view with special reference to peopling and structure' Partha P Majumdar, Anabala Basu et al.ISI Calcutta)

3.5 Whatever may be the case, the meaning of caste changed much. For example, in the words of the certain early writer, "No caste was originally considered superior or inferior, except in the sense that its body type represented a more or less advanced stage in human habitations which must be, in turn, occupied by the soul". But now it has assumed a more powerful role: one dividing people into, groups with different responsibilities, functions, and rights, i.e., different societies altogether. (Indian Antiquary, March 1930, Origin of the Caste system in India- S Charles Hill)

3.6 Endogamy, as well as measures instituted by the invading group in governing the land, might be able to put forth a rationale for the development of caste; however fails in providing a reasonable explanation to the fact that we have myriad of castes, each having perceptible differences in ability when compared with one another.

Chapter 4

EVOLUTION OF CASTE – A REVIEW

4.1 Whatever the shape, the evolution of caste took; it certainly resulted in a large multitude of castes. And notably, these castes were showing easily discernible differences, especially on one's aims, aspirations, and matters of intellectual ability when compared with one another. As we have seen earlier, all the theories of formation and development of caste fail in providing a satisfactory explanation for this phenomenon.

4.2 This could have been caused by peculiar circumstances of the evolution of Indian society, mainly owing to the changes brought in by external stimuli, two of such being:

-Foreign occupation. Conquests by Muslims, Europeans and the British, and lately,

-The Russian revolution, various mass movements of eastern Europe, and China.

And the Indian thought came under the influence of different ideas, like communism.

As a result of these, caste became entrenched in Indian society, the stratification property offering much convenience in administration, where each caste is a form of the disciplined guild. And for the society at large, the structural constitution of the castes started to provide a stable force in the direction of prosperity, members of each caste having more or less assured opportunities of earning a livelihood.

It should be remembered that Indian philosophical thought places much importance on abstract matters like one's duty, status, or rebirth. Caste being one such idea, a conceptual step of stratification might not have caused much consternation in everyday life, while meeting the self-actualization needs (and similar top level ones in the hierarchy of human wants) of ancient Indian society. As mentioned at many places in ancient Indian literature (Dharmasastra), the overriding need of the people was to attain a desirable status in their next birth. Due to this reason, the populace at large was unconcerned about comforts of life even in the activities involved with daily subsistence; or rather the present life itself was of secondary nature, as long as the list of reckon-able deeds in each one's account is kept at a comfortably high level. Added to this is the fact that no ancient text fail to bring out the importance of doing ones job as dictated by one's caste duties, to attain a desirably better status in next life.

All these might have succeeded in instilling an otherwise unfathomable degree of indifference in each, such that nobody found it necessary either to force ones caste privileges or to react to the disagreeable impositions of caste.

3.3 That many parts of India, such as parts of Himachal Pradesh, northeast including Assam and some parts of central India appear to have been having village communes, where all forms of labor were valued equally, probably points to the nonexistence of any form of caste-like discrimination. Also, it may be worth noting that, caste-like divisions are found in the history of most nations, in the American continent, Africa, Europe or elsewhere in Asia, some societies having complex divisions and others' relatively simple. Samurais and priests of early Japan and feudal lords of Europe are examples of social systems having stratification as well as hereditary progression, in the lines of the caste system of India. Over and above this, a few among these nations could also boast of still greater social inequalities manifested in institution of slavery, a cruel practice, if not worse.

4.4 And that 'untouchability', which finds no place in Indian history, is mentioned in the history of Herodotus, "the pig is regarded among them as an unclean animal... are forbidden entry to any of the temples... and no one will give his daughter in marriage to a swineherd or take a wife from among them so that swineherds are forced to intermarry among themselves", further supports this view. (see 'The history of Herodotus', Book I CLIO Translated by George Rawlinson http://classics.mit.edu/Herodotus/history.html)

4.5 In short, Indian society, which welcomed the first invader, was culturally a fully developed one having certain abstract notions of stratification encompassing all aspects of life and society. Thus we have categories or different types of, men, women, guests, maidens, horses, dogs, cows, other things like plants, activities like sleeping, other abstractions like friends, enemies and others with further subdivisions leading to myriad of arcane classifications, each possessing unique functional attributes; caste being one such theme of classification.

Such an abstract nature of caste will be even more clear, if we are to note that ancient Hindu texts contain many instances where the moral worth of a person is shown to be having greater importance compared to other attributes, say caste or family background. For example, it says, "truthfulness, generosity, restraint, tapas, constant adherence to dharma- these always lead men to fruition (of their goal) and not caste nor family", or "Truthfulness, generosity, freedom from hatred, humility, kindness, and tapas- he is known as Brahmana where all these are seen", and also, "if these qualities can be seen in a Sudra, but do not exist in a Brahmana, the Sudra would not be a Sudra and the Brahmana would not be a Brahmana"

Chapter 5

PROGRESSION OF CASTE – A SCRUTINY

5.1 Before British: Early invasions to India, almost all of them, resulted in establishing an Islamic rule in India which created "a much stronger and much unified elite, which made it difficult for the ordinary masses to resist social changes, particularly in the realm of philosophical choice, religious pluralism, and other personal preferences" Notion of sexual prudery and gender separation infected Hindu households as well. The cultural, military and political intercourse with the early invaders does not seem to have made any other mark of more permanent nature on Indian society. Neither did it have a revolutionary impact on Hindu society to alter the equitable social relations drastically.

5.2 Long before the arrival of Islam, new religious or reform movements within India opposed many of the social customs. In 6th century BC, Buddhism started it. On caste system as a whole, how much of an effect Buddhism could produce is not known. In fact, the very nature of caste in the early days is not clearly identified. For example, John W McCrindle mentions in his book 'Ancient India as described by Megastanese and Arrian', "According to Megastanes, race of India is divided into seven castes".

1 Philosophers- Only they are allowed to marry outside caste.

2 Husbandmen- They cultivate land

3 Herdsmen and hunters- They lead a wandering life

4 Tradesmen- They work in trades like weapon making

5 Fighting men

6 Overseers- They conduct general supervision and report to king

7 Assessors and councilors- They conduct justice, public matters etc"

As another example, castes are mentioned to be resulting from "the intermingling of 'varna's". (Inscriptions of Nepal' DR Rajmi) Some authors go beyond that, to mention that although "each caste has its own dharma (calling), the conduct is less rigid than it has been since Moslem invasions". ('Asoka- His history' Vincent Smith)

5.3 Effects of British ascendancy: In the beginning, the British did not make any attempt to interfere with the caste system prevailing in India. In his observations on India, 'The future results of British rule in India', New York Daily Tribune, 8 August 1853, Karl Marx writes "The village isolation produced the absence of roads in India and the absence of roads perpetuated the village isolation. On this plan a community existed with a given scale of low conveniences, almost without intercourse with other villages, and without the desires and efforts indispensable to social advance". The British, by bringing steam and railways into India initiated regular and rapid communication. Further introduction of roads breaking up the "self-sufficient inertia" of Indian villages are some of the effects of British rule, though aimed at confiscating from India wealth in every possible form while forbidding at the same time propagation of ideas which might not have been favorable for such ends. "The modern industry resulting from railway system will dissolve the hereditary divisions of labor, upon which rests the Indian castes".

But that did not take place. True, changes in the social atmosphere resulted in the rapid progress of the industrial sphere. But, instead of causing any improvements to Indian society, all those moves got absorbed quietly. It happened so, since each such move got appropriated to suit the ordering of caste system.

5.4 In a paper 'The Indian caste system and the British ethnographic mapping', (www.infinityfoundation.com/ECITcastebritishframeset.htm) Kevin Hobson says, "The caste system had been a fascination of the British since their arrival in India. Coming from a society that was divided by class, the British attempted to equate the caste system to the class system." As late as 1937, Professor TC Hodson stated that: 'Class and caste stand to each other in the relation of family to species. The general classification is by classes, the detailed one by castes. The former represents the external, the latter the internal view of the social organization.' The difficulty with definitions such as this is that class is based on political and economic factors, caste is not. In fairness to Professor Hodson, by the time of his writing, caste had taken on many of the characteristics that he ascribed to it in addition to the ones already attributed by his predecessors, but during the 19th-century caste was not what the British believed it to be. It did not constitute a rigid description of the occupation and social level of a given group and it did not bear any real resemblance to the class system. However, this will be dealt with later in this essay.

At present, the main concern is that the British saw caste as a way to manage a huge population by breaking it down into discrete chunks, each having specific characteristics and an inbuilt disciplinary structure. Moreover, it appears that the caste system extant in the late 19th and early 20th century has been altered as a result of British actions so that it increasingly took on the features that were ascribed to by the British. What the British failed to realize was that the Hindus existed in a different cosmological frame than did the British. "The concern of the true Hindu was not his ranking economically within society but rather his ability to regenerate on a higher plane of existence during each successive life" ('The Indian caste system and the British- Ethnographic mapping and the construction of the British census in India')

He goes on to say that a census was undertaken in India, in 1872 for the first time, as one of the main tools used in the British attempt to understand Indian population. The census forced the Indian social system into a written schematic in a way that had never been experienced in the past. While the Mughals had issued written decrees on the status of individual castes, there had never been a formal systematic attempt to organize and schedule all of the castes in an official document until the advent of the British census. The data was compiled on the British understanding of India.

Based on the census results, the British formed certain notions about Indian society and these notions led to the classification of intelligence and abilities based on physical attributes and this, in turn, led to employment opportunities being limited to certain caste groupings that displayed the appropriate attributes. Indians attempted to incorporate themselves into this evolving system by organizing caste 'sabhas' with the purpose of attaining improved status within the system. This ran contrary to the traditional purpose of the caste system and imposed an economic basis. With this, the relevance and importance of the spiritual, non-material rationale for caste were degraded and caste took a far more material meaning. In a sense, caste became politicized as decisions regarding caste increasingly fell into political rather than the spiritual sphere of influence. "With this politicization, caste moved closer to class in connotation... In expropriating the knowledge base of Indian society, the British had forced Indian society and caste system to execute adjustments in order to prosper within the rubric of the British regime".

Thus we can see that caste was appropriated and in many respects reinvented by the British to create what it is now, a social stratification system of convenience with Brahman clearly at the head. That such was not the case in earlier times is mentioned, among others, by Dr. Subhash Sharma, who says that "the evolution of the society and customs were mainly due to individual and collective needs and choices. In addition, role and influence of various espoused or suggested proclamations such as involving 'varnasrama dharma, manusmriti', on the development and progress of society at large was rather insignificant." (see http://kellog.nd.edu/events/pdfs/Jaffrelot.pdf)

Chapter 6

CASTE AND NATIONALIST MOVEMENTS -

AN APPRAISAL

6.1 History of India is replete with stories of social moderation efforts or other rearrangements, that too of a permanent nature, frequently necessitated in a non-homogeneous society, if it is to continue intact. In the early times, if Buddhism and Jainism heralded such efforts, we have Sikhism of relatively recent origin, all forerunners of social reformists. Raja Rammohan Roy, who could be called the father of Hindu reformation, gave leadership to Hindu revival in modern times. Dayanand Saraswati and Arya Samaj, Annie Besant and Theosophical society, Ramakrishna, Swami Vivekananda are some of those great ones who tried to cut through the sectarian lines of Indian religious organization, whose life and times certainly had been a source of inspiration for such efforts during the freedom movement. However, those not belonging to upper castes, on becoming members realized that these organizations were primarily concerned with the resurgence of Hinduism rather than reform, as exemplified in the case of Swami Achyuthanand, one of the important scheduled caste leaders of UP in 1920-30, who was a member of Arya Samaj. (see http://kellog.nd.edu/events/pdfs/Jaffrelot.pdf)

The Untouchables and other low castes resorted to 'low caste movements' of various nature. Such social movements can be broadly classified into two groups, those advocating resilience on the part of followers, mainly those of upper caste, and those suggesting adjustments in practice of caste system to include egalitarian precepts. One can also find an exception here - Mahatma Gandhi's views on social struggle.

6.2 Mahatma Gandhi's views, about caste and the many facets of such social 'ills', underwent a gradual change, from 1920's to late 1940's.

-In 1920, he believed in the inevitability of caste system. He also held that the many fruits that Indian society reaped over centuries were mainly owing to this. As examples, "I believe that caste has saved Hinduism from disintegration", (Mahatma Gandhi, the collected works' Delhi(58-94) Vol XIX p 83) or, "In accepting the fourfold division, I am accepting the laws of nature" (Vol XXIX p 410) can be quoted.

-By mid 20's, he would start downplaying the inevitability of natural division, "In my conception of the law of 'varna', no one is superior to any other... A scavenger has the same status as a Brahmin" (Vol XXXV p 260)

-As the 30's reached, he started observing that "unequal economic and social status perhaps existed, over the ages, and we have to enrich the inheritance left to us" (Vol LIX p 319) and by 1935, "caste has to go. The sooner the public opinion abolishes it, the better" (Vol LXII p 121)

-In 1940, he started expressing the importance of marriages between 'atishudras' and caste Hindus. From according "highest importance to marriages between atishudras and caste Hindus" (Vol LXXX p 77) and declaring that he will bless a couple "if the girl is from another community only" (Vol LXXX p 99), he reached,

-by 1945, understanding inter-caste as well as inter-religious marriage (if necessary, civil marriages), as a welcome reform, and

-by 1947, he welcomed "inter-religious marriages whenever it took place" (Vol LXIV p 35)

Had it not been for his assassination, we would have been witnessing Indian society, more as Mahatma Gandhi expressed on numerous occasions, "entire Hindu society converted to my view" (Vol LXLI p 318)

6.3 Thus we see that, as part of nationalistic movements, there were sporadic activities initiated from all directions for moderating the practice of caste system. However, the absence of concerted efforts or a specific aim failed to channelize this, resulting in no substantive changes in the overall appearance of caste.

The path caste took, during the birth of free India and her democracy can now be summed up as a half-hearted attempt at the generation of an egalitarian society. Whether in relation to the history of gender, the victimization of Dalits, the rise of anti-Brahmin feelings and backward caste politics, or other social problems that was predominant in post-British India, caste has worked to compromise whatever good work that took place for national unity and is a part of India's civilized history. Caste has become the focus of progressive movements and of debates about the character of postcolonial politics. In fact in a debate on any issue, if 'caste' is part of the discussion, any of the participants can turn the current issue to one of oppression, conflict, or other matters related to 'caste'. Which enables one to make easily and at will, changes to the very course of discussion, taking it away from whatever one may feel inconvenient about.

It has also become the uncomfortable reminder that all claims about community are claims about privilege, participation, and exclusion... "caste has simultaneously preserved the patriarchy of pre-modern society and worked to sanction the continued oppression and exclusion of women in nationalist re-imaginings of the past. Caste may be the precipitate of the modern, but it is still the specter of the past" (see http://press.princeton.edu/chapters/s7191.html)

Chapter 7

CASTE – MY SIDE – The Singularities

While studying the origins of the caste system, a rather silly but grave mistake seems to have crept into all the theories mentioned earlier without anybody noticing it. Almost all experts take caste merely as a 'rigid social class into which members are born and from which they can escape or withdraw with extreme difficulty'. None of the doctrines takes cognizance of the philosophical plane of existence of caste. (Referring to caste as 'varna', an abstraction)

I think the efforts taken by some authors (see 'Caste class and race' Oliver Cromwell Cox) for simplifying this by proposing that 'castes are hardened form of social classes' did lead to the incorrect surmise that 'the upper caste might have been formed from the existing higher classes of the society'. Presenting a seemingly accurate answer to one very significant question anyone trying to understand caste would have been hoping to solve, this deduction, rather a hasty guess, effectively puts a brake to any study in this regard. Such conjectures are, in addition, very dangerous, not only that these do not show how the abstract 'varna' metamorphosed into iniquitous 'caste', but also introduce a material status to castes which the 'varna' doesn't have. This surmise is so simple and plausible is the reason that the true essence of caste, its conceptual plane of existence, got relegated to the background.

With that, we started to rate castes as low or high. Naturally, we followed it up by rating as superior or inferior, whatever was the respective occupation of people of those castes. (This explains why we have a more or less specified amount of an abstract value, 'status', attached to each and every job, pastimes, or other entertainments!)

The comparison between these two is further hindered by the fact that unlike castes, social classes, of course present in any society, are not founded upon occupational limitation. The class should be thought of as something presenting the external view of social organization, and caste, 'the internal, abstract view'.

While examining the ancient texts of India for this study, what stood out was the distinctive approach of our forefathers, who spent much time and effort in 'classification' as a primary step towards learning new things or for greater understanding. Thus we have all objects, animate or inanimate, all actions and other abstractions classified into esoteric groups and subgroups, each having identifiable qualities. Many methods are mentioned about stratification, for example, of men and women into 'varna' based on intellectual orientation, of women into different types based on disposition of their social nature, of liquor into different types, namely Medaka, Prasanna, Asava, Arista, Maitreya, and Madhu based on the manufacturing process, of all activities of war and love, based on numerous such parameters. Ancient texts like 'Kamasutra of Vatsyayana and 'Arthsastra' of 'Chanakya' contain many dissertations on such topics.

For example, see what is given in 'Arthsastra' regarding sons:

The son begotten by a man on his wife who has gone through all the required ceremonials is called aurasa, natural son; equal to him is the son of an appointed daughter (putrikáputra); the son begotten on the wife by another man, appointed for the purpose, and of the same gotra as that of the husband; or of a different gotra, is called kshetraja; on the death of the begetter, the kshetraja son will be the son to both the fathers, follow the gotras of both, offer funeral libations to both, and take possession of the immovable property (ríktha) of both of them; of the same status as the kshetraja is he who is secretly begotten in the house of relatives and is called gúdhaja, secretly born; the son cast off by his natural parents is called apaviddha and will belong to that man who performs necessary religious ceremonials to him; the son born of a maiden (before wedlock) is called kánína; the son born of a woman married while carrying is called sahodha; the son of a remarried woman (punarbhátáyáh.) is called paunarbhava. A natural son can claim relationship both with his father and his father's relatives, but a son born to another man can have a relationship only with his adopter. Of the same status as the latter is he who is given in adoption with water by both the father and mother and is called datta. The son who, either of his own accord or following the intention of his relatives, offers himself to be the son of another, is called upagata. He who is appointed as a son is called kritaka; and he who is purchased is called kríta.

Or, see another example of what 'Kama Sutra' of Vatsyayana tells about love:

Men learned in the humanities are of opinion that love is of four kinds, viz.:

Love acquired by continual habit.

Love resulting from the imagination.

Love resulting from belief.

Love resulting from the perception of external objects.

(1). Love resulting from the constant and continual performance and habit, as for instance the love of sexual intercourse, the love of hunting, the love of drinking, the love of gambling, etc., etc.

(2). Love which is felt for things to which we are not habituated, and which proceeds entirely from ideas, is called love resulting from imagination, as for instance, that love which some men and women and eunuchs feel for the Auparishtaka or mouth congress, and that which is felt by all for such things as embracing, kissing, etc., etc.

(3). The love which is mutual on both sides, and proved to be true, when each looks upon the other as his or her very own, such is called love resulting from the belief by the learned.

(4). The love resulting from the perception of eternal objects is quite evident and well-known to the world because the pleasure which it affords is superior to the pleasure of the other kinds of love, which exists only for its sake.

It, therefore, stands to reason, if we are to consider 'varna', or 'caste' also, as just another style of classification. This style of classification is adopted for better organization, easier management and real-time monitoring of the populace. Interestingly, the complete populace takes an active part in governing themselves, greatly easing the burden of governance, while invoking self esteem. (Which perhaps could be seen as another indicator of the superior standards of the ancient Indian society)

Whether in later writings or in social customs, no evidence can be seen pointing to the establishment and practice of these romantic delineations in daily living. On the contrary, discourses pointing to the abstract nature of many such divisions, with caste being a prominent one among them, can be seen at many places in our old texts. For example, Chanakya Niti Shastra specifies detailed directions for attributing different caste status to citizens. A sample of such instructions is shown below which reasserts this view.

"The brahmana who is engrossed in worldly affairs brings up cows and is engaged in trade is called a vaishya. The brahmana who deals with lac-die, articles, oil, indigo, silken cloth, honey, clarified butter, liquor or flesh is called a shudra." (see Chanakya Niti Shastra, translated by Miles Davis http://indiadivine.com)

In fact, the abundance of exhortations and references pointing to the conceptual plane of existence of caste makes one wonder, were our forefathers making it unambiguous and clear that 'caste' should never be confused with anything but the abstract? Perhaps, they could foresee the tumultuous times ahead for the society, if people mistook caste as something to do with real life?

While reflecting on the nature of caste system, each and every historian, researcher or reformer seem to have been deeply influenced by certain peculiarity or individuality exhibited by one odd facet of its practice leading them to overlook all the other aspects. That is, almost all authors who have written about caste in India are profligate when it comes to elaborating the many and varied forms in which it does manifest, but thrifty when describing the unique internal structure of caste, in which it does perpetuate freely and effortlessly. (It seems all those who approached the issue of caste, especially in modern times, were either an opponent or a supporter of this setup. There is plenty of literature, ancient as well as modern, discussing the merits or the demerits of the caste system in detail. Hardly any could be found, for a balanced or unbiased view)

A different view, which was espoused by Mahatma Gandhi, mentions only the inner, abstract element of caste, forgetting the many unwelcome, irrational and unjust elements of its practice.

A still different view is being presented in the following pages, in an attempt to combine both the facets of caste, the internal as well as the external. Which is based on a presumption: of the countless treasure of esoteric divisions and themes, the ancient texts contain, caste alone happened to get instituted into our society. This presumption is further examined in the light of two facts. One, many and varied social institutions existed in other nations as well, with the capacity to cause large-scale oppression. For example, heresy, inquisition or lynching. Two, over time, all of these transformed smoothly into its modern versions, whereas, caste continues to survive here with its oppressive potential largely unchanged.

That naturally should be leading one to the conclusion that caste found its way into the modern day society owing to the 'singularities', during the evolution of social life in India. Or whatever were the peculiarities that differentiated Indian society from rest of the world and contributed handsomely to the evolution of society. These 'singularities' could also be the reason which prevented caste from meeting its natural end along with contemporary social edifices of other societies.

(I think it is not at all easy to identify such a singularity. For those of this society, it may not present a deviation from the norm. For those from another society, each singularity could hide among other more notable but less potent traits of character.)

7.1 The very first singularity is philosophy or the way it is understood by the society at large. For example, societies (Indian philosophy in particular and others in general) treat possessions as unnecessary, or at least as overvalued additions to one's life. These also bring misery to man, which in effect lead to a state, where, lesser the possessions, more desirable the life becomes.

This is not as harmless a thought, as it looks. We, I think, do not realize that the story of the progress, human species have achieved so far, is the story of our efforts, in adding new possessions, in retaining a few or in the destruction of some. Further, this did lead, as Marx observed earlier, to the formation of caste as the result of 'the total lack of social intercourse' compounded by 'absence of desires and efforts indispensable to social advance'. This lack of social intercourse can be easily attributed to the possibility that the society that flourished in India in the ancient times would have been remarkably calm and totally self-sufficient. Also, the populace, which is always at an equilibrium induced by philosophy would not have been finding a reason worthy enough to cause agitation.

In fact, this will be much clear if we compare the importance of the part played by philosophy in the conduct of life and the activities that make it, to the role played by a spring and dashpot mechanism in a traditional mechanical system or that played by a capacitor-inductor combination in a similar electrical system. These arrangements are provided to dampen disturbances, and thereby enable smooth operation of the particular system.

As it is well known, failure can happen in any system due to a mechanical or physical shock, which is a sudden acceleration or deceleration, caused, for example, by impact, drop, a kick or other design deficiency. Failure can also be caused by an electrical shock, for example, by lightning, overload or short circuit, that can cause a sudden change in the electrical parameters. (voltage, current, frequency etc)

That can result in abrupt changes in operating conditions, which can lead to system failure, or malfunction, or both.

In a mechanical system, the spring-dashpot arrangement introduces stability in its operation by absorbing sudden changes in acceleration. As far as an electrical system goes, the capacitor-inductor combination cancels out the instantaneous changes in the values of voltage (absorbed by the capacitor) and current (blocked by the inductor), thereby preventing the system from any abrupt changes caused by disturbances. This is how we ensure smooth operation of both the systems.

It should be remembered that such mechanisms are noticeable by its absence in systems which are expected to perform beyond conventional limits, like the control mechanism of a supersonic fighter aircraft. A high-performance system should be designed to accept large disturbances in the signal and it cannot afford to have such 'smoothing' incorporated. Or, as a corollary, a system protected from such large disturbances cannot operate beyond conventional limits or attain high performance.

To apply this argument to human society, remember that philosophy, being the smoothing force of a culture, inhibits any sudden changes in the behavior or outlook of the people, in response to external or internal stimuli. Not only that, systems of education follow a society's philosophic ideas about what children should be taught and for what purposes. Some societies may stress that young people learn to think and make choices for themselves. Few others may discourage any such activity and would want their youth to surrender their own interests to those of the state. A few others would like to live in the memories of past glory, encouraging the youth to assess every new turn with such a yardstick for acceptance or rejection. The values and skills taught by the educational system of a society thus reflect the society's philosophic ideas of what is important.

Thus we can easily see, philosophy helps people to clarify what they believe, and they can be stimulated to think about ultimate questions, beliefs about what is important, true, real, and significant. It thus makes life immune to any type of disorder or disturbance in the society, which might have been due to external or internal aggression or natural or unnatural causes.

Whenever destructive disturbances arise, it is the smoothing character of philosophy that keeps a society from disintegration and despair. (One who has a matured outlook do not fall easily to novel ideas) On the contrary, societies that are not philosophically oriented shall be led quickly to their doom, since people from those societies are likely to jump to any novel idea. Or, wherever disturbances arise, it is the smoothing character of philosophy that shall keep a society from destroying itself.

When the 'disturbance' is due to something benevolent, say a new invention or turbulence resulting from a desirable social change, societies that are void in philosophical support adapt to such changes quickly, reaping the associated benefits. Those societies which are philosophically well ahead refuse to get disturbed, thus failing to harvest any benefit of the change. (Many a time, such societies may not find anything 'beneficial' in a change, being already in a state of bliss)

It should be noted that doom, as well as progress, involve change, and philosophy, by inhibiting change, immunizes a society from both. Therefore we can say that to progress, we should be ready to tolerate disorder, the more willing we are in accommodating disturbances, the faster shall be our progress. Or we can say, wherever constructive disturbances arose, it was the smoothing character of philosophy that kept a society from reaping its benefit.

This is what happened. Caste-like divisions, which would have been of use once upon a time, continued to remain in Indian society as it was safely guarded by philosophy against any kind of influence that would have led to changes.

7.2 Next singularity is the invaders, traders or explorers whose attacks, interactions or findings did make long-standing impacts. Almost all of them contributed handsomely to changes in the social appearance of the caste system, some of them due to their inability in comprehending the uniqueness of Indian caste system and others by their cleverness in shaping the caste system to suit the needs of governing the vanquished. British, though had the longest lasting empire in India, in fact, did nothing to alter the existing caste equations or to restructure the society for the better. Not only that, they seem to have made considerable efforts towards bringing the material aspect of caste differences to fore to enjoy temporal benefits.

This stands in stark opposition to their efforts in the direction of the welfare of Aborigines and their integration in another part of British Empire, Australia. Which is quite striking, since further studies clearly show that "several of the tribes of southern India, who were of the race 'Homo Dravida', had more in common with Australian aboriginals than their Aryan or high caste neighbors" (see Race, Caste and Tribe in Central India: the early origins of Indian anthropometry - Crispin Bates http://www.csas.ed.ac.uk/fichiers/BATES_RaceCaste&Tribe.pdf)

To cite an example of the thoughtful steps, some of the colonial administrators took, "When Dr. Cecil Cook was appointed Chief Protector in 1927; he was wholly unsupportive of the missions. This was partly because of the poor conditions. More importantly, Cook had a similar vision of assimilation as West Australian Chief Protector A.O.

Neville. Cook supported biological assimilation. Generally by the fifth and invariably by the sixth generation, all native characteristics of the Australian aborigine are eradicated. The problem of our half-castes will quickly be eliminated by the complete disappearance of the black race, and the swift submergence of their progeny in the white" (see *Bringing them home - The History*

http://www.hreoc.gov.au/bth/text_versions/map/history/nt.html)
(Note: In Australia, there is no single Aboriginal "traditional" culture, it varies in time and place. Over 400 tribes, each with their own language and traditions, have been found to constitute the aborigines. Moreover, certain aspects of culture found in one region may be absent in others. It is possible that some practices described may only occur in some areas, by particular tribes (also called "language groups" or "nations"), or by particular people. In this sense, it is quite possible that in the natural course, Australia would have become a group of nations, just as Europe is today.)

The British, even though appreciated problems of black race, half-caste as well as native characteristics and took appropriate corrective actions as and when they encountered those issues in Australia, found that, when it came to India, caste system is a great expedient which could be put to effective use in the governance of that country. In appropriating the caste system for their use, not only that they chose to overlook all the ills associated with it, but also planned their further moves to derive whatever benefits it offered. All the chroniclers of British Empire seem to have glossed over this conundrum, by a mere acknowledgment that the diversity of races in India and the presence of a powerful Mohammedan community greatly favored the maintenance of 'our' rule.

To put briefly, it needs to be noted that all the available discourses on the history of caste in India fail to provide a logical explanation for two historical facts. The British, who identified certain problems connected with caste-like divisions in the Australian part of their empire, realized that those are detrimental to a healthy society, suggested solutions for its eradication and passed suitable laws to implement them. The same British, when in the Indian part of their empire encountered more severe caste issues, not only overlooked the ills but also strengthened the social presence of 'caste' further and made it more spread out. And by according status and acceptability to it, they ended up converting caste into a coveted social attribute.

As a result of this enhanced social relevance, caste status of each and every individual started to influence various benefits that are to accrue to one in the material plane. This altered the traditional meaning of caste. From the abstract and harmless 'varna' with its say on the equally harmless matters of rebirth, caste became one of great significance to current life. This resulted in certain radical changes, which continued ever since. A more earthly meaning came to be associated with caste and it started establishing itself as a social division of permanence as time went by.

Had this (rather than remaining as a convenience for ceremonial purity, caste acquiring an earthly meaning) not happened, the whole gamut of delineating people into different 'varna' would have been taking its rightful place along with all other abstract, esoteric divisions like eight types of marriages, four types of sleep or seven types of teachers. To show one such grouping, elephants are studied in seven functional, objective divisions:

i) Which lets a man mount over it when in company with another elephant (kunjaropaváhya)

ii) Which can be used for riding when led by a warlike elephant (sánnáhyopaváhya)

iii) Which is taught trotting (dhorana)

iv) Which is taught various kinds of movements (ádhánagatika)

v) Which can be made to move by using a staff (yashtyupaváhya)

vi) Which can be made to move by using an iron hook (totropaváhya)

vii) Which can be made to move without whips (suddhopaváhya)

(as prescribed by Arthsastra)

All this brings us to a question. Why did the British fiddle with the Indian caste system without realizing its full magnitude and essence, a rather uncharacteristic move from a great culture? Had they not done it, caste would have been remaining as just another matter of academic interest leaving hardly any room for consternation other than for pedantic one-upmanship.

7.3 Another singularity took the form of Mahatma Gandhi. His views contained advice unfavorable to caste lovers, such as, "I believe in 'varnashrama' of the Vedas which is based on absolute equality of status, notwithstanding passages to the contrary elsewhere", "The most effective, quickest, and the most unobtrusive way to destroy caste is for reformers to begin the practice with themselves" and "The higher classes will have to descend from their pedestal" (Vol LXII p 121)

His advice to the lower caste was that they should "endeavor to merge themselves in the ocean of Hindu community" and "trust merit to command attention" (Vol LVIII p 163) On another occasion, he is seen as proclaiming that reserving seats (for positions) is a dangerous principle. "Protection of neglected classes should not be carried to an extent which will harm them... and a person after he has secured a seat in an elected body should depend upon his intrinsic merit and popularity to secure coveted positions" (Vol LXXVI p 314) To the "castemen", on the other hand, his advice was that they "should prove that they had obliterated caste by their readiness to take up all those occupations which the 'untouchables' engaged in. Thus they should be ready to do scavengers' work. The system of cleaning toilets would then be automatically transformed. In England, real Bhangis were famous engineers and sanitarians... who had a perfectly clean way of dealing with human excreta... Needless to say, the Harijans will live in the same streets as others without any segregation..."

Given that the prestige and influence associated with the name Mahatma Gandhi were, at that time, an all-time high, above mentioned changes would have taken place, leading to a massive social revolution. That would have resulted in the future as he hoped for, leading to a new India with a greater degree of cohesion in society, upper caste much less 'upper' and lower caste none 'lower' than any other. A two-pronged strategy can be seen to have been put in place by those of the upper castes to obfuscate such 'preposterous' suggestions of Mahatma Gandhi, the acceptance of which would certainly have resulted in them or their progeny (for sure) to have lost their exclusiveness. (which caste status brought)

Firstly, while drafting a new constitution, introduce social and political changes which will have the potential for cementing the caste divisions with added strength. Towards this end, a certain provision like, reservation for low caste people is introduced with the apparent aim of dealing with the caste problem.

For their luck, the idea of reservation was readily adopted by the framers of the Indian constitution, obviously without much meaningful debate. (see *http://parliamentofindia.nic.in/ls/debates/*)

This perhaps points to the dire need, then existed, for finding a via-media to the suggestions of Mahatma Gandhi. Though there were opposing sounds as can be seen in a couple of discussions shown below, these were not forceful enough to make a mark.

  1 Pandit Thakur Dass Bhargava: opposes reservation during the debates while discussing art 294 of Indian constitution. "...... it may be said that in wealth, social influence and social status they are inferior, but all the same I want that their position may be leveled up in ways other than by reservation of seats... will be very harmful..." (see *http://parliamentofindia.nic.in/ls/debates/vol7p3b.htm*)

  2 Shri Brajeshwar Prasad: "...The problems (the scheduled castes face) are primarily educational and of an economic character. They are of a cultural character. We want to raise the cultural level of these down-trodden and oppressed people. I do not see how their representation in the legislatures will in any way alter the material and the moral level of these people. Representations here and there will provide opportunities for a handful of leaders but it will not in any way materially alter their economic or their educational level. Better lay down in the Constitution that a fixed percentage in the budget, both Central and Provincial, shall be exclusively devoted for their welfare...I am quite clear in my own mind that by giving them a few seats here and there, their economic condition and their education level will in no way be   improved"   (see http://parliamentofindia.nic.in/ls/debates/vol9p17b.htm)

Secondly, rather than a shrewd and intelligent social reformer whose words should carry more weight than his figure, the very image evoked by the name Mahatma Gandhi was altered such that the people are made to see a saintly visage whose form is immensely loveable, everything else paling into insignificance. To achieve this, a silent but effective method was put into motion. All that Mahatma Gandhi ever wrote, specifically on abstract topics (on such intangibles like truth, love etc) is given wide publicity while condemning to obscurity, all his writings on other earthly topics, most of which dealing with caste issues and Harijan welfare, that too, in many places with concrete suggestions. The incongruity of idolizing Mahatma Gandhi as the father of nation while ignoring almost everything he mentioned about the nation and its soul however remains.

However, everyone took to heart one opinion of the Mahatma, that low caste brethren needs our love. Through this perspective, reservation could be seen (still so!) as a sacrifice forced on the upper caste population while providing incomparable benefits to those of lower castes. No wonder, support for reservation was huge. Also, any opinion against 'reservation' could be easily construed as something aimed to weaken the lower castes.

7.4 Communism presented itself, indirectly though, as another singularity. This sphere of thought, especially the revolutions it gave birth to, in Russia and China, could have deeply influenced Indian leaders. The resulting social order of equality would have greatly influenced our appreciation of caste issues and the way we are to find answers to the problems it posed.

Its potential to spark long-standing changes in the social environment will be amply clear if we are to note that communism in fact sports more than one face. What we commonly see, a group of young (and maybe not so young) men and women charged with ideals and the desire to see the 'plight' of many changed for the better, is one. A group (this may be a smaller one) of 'intellectuals' who manufacture propositions convincing enough to inspire, propel and guide them in their quest, making them move forward with incessant thrust, is the other. The former is responsible for all that we welcome in a change, the alacrity, the selfless devotion of protagonists and absence of any motive or consanguineous profit other than for the benefit of all. In short, in communism, those who follow the precepts are the best of humanity and the system sometimes produce good results even though the philosophy is flawed. Also, as this happened in societies already hitting the rock bottom, something favorable could be seen in every result achieved. Which might be the reason that no one noticed the contradictions it contained, till communism collapsed.

During communism in Russia, the famines of 1921 and 1932-33 resulted in the death of more 5 million people each (Not counting additional deaths of 7-8 million people in the violence involved with 'dekulakization' during the period 1930-37) Also, the state policies of agriculture in Russia, as well as China, was based on 'lysenkoism', a modified form of Lamarck's theories, some of the main beliefs of which is that, like species help each other whereas unlike species do not, as well as, inheritance of acquired characteristics.

In China too, communists adopted such principles in guiding state farming policy. Accordingly, Mao ordered, organizing the agriculture into collectives, introducing certain farming practices like close planting, deep plowing, nonuse of chemical fertilizer etc, resulting in massive fall in agricultural output giving rise to a famine on a scale never before seen in China. In the period 1958-61, acute food shortage resulted in the death of a staggering 30 to 40 million Chinese.

The invisible bond that held people of each caste together, especially in times of need, was the factor which insulated the Indian society from the effects of global changes. This I think is the reason, the barbaric period of The Middle Ages failed to leave any tell-tale mark in India. Over the recent past, communism also, like any other global movement, did not succeed in making any direct impact or lasting changes on Indian society, even though 'Lysenkoism' and the possibility of inheriting environmentally acquired characteristics proposed by that theory found its way into the hearts of the 'reservationists', providing them with the necessary scientific foundation to propagate the idea of 'reservation' as a panacea for all social inequalities. In fact, this scientific foundation is the reason why many progressives continued to support reservation as a vehicle of growth.

(see   http://www.overpopulation.com/faq/health/hunger/famine, http://www.galafilm.com/afterdarwin/english/glossary/

lysenkoism.html, http://www.softpanorama.org/Skeptics/lysenkoism.shtml)

7.5 Next singularity, the most potent of all, is reservation or its euphemism, social justice. The romantic thought, of lower caste brethren being uplifted en masse, by a tiny adaptation on the part of those belonging to the upper caste, must have influenced our constitution makers. Otherwise, it is impossible to justify such a serious lapse as overlooking the most substantial side effect. That, this shall result in perpetuating caste system.

The desirable changes reservation system did bring in, and is doing so have been discussed at length, the general idea emerging from all these is that reservation system offers many advantages to the downtrodden, marginalized sections. The only disadvantage of reservation system is that (mainly) opportunity is being curtailed for upper caste people, that is to say,

- Advantages of 'reservation' shall be exclusive to those lower in caste, and

- Disadvantages of 'reservation' shall be directed exclusively to those higher in caste.

Such an idea is preposterous. Reservation system may be providing certain advantages to the marginalized sections, however, some disadvantages also are their share. The most severe one among such impediments is that it reduces or takes away the requirement of competing. To be specific, it nullifies the necessity for engaging in a contest with people of other castes. As a result of which, everyone lower in caste is denied a better opponent, the best catalyst for growth. As competition is removed from those of lower caste, they also are denied the fruits of competition, the sweetest of which, as is well known, is all-round development including intellectual acuity, the most important fruit.

Thus the most substantial, lasting effect of reservation is that, for those who get reserved positions, further growth also gets stunted in all dimensions. (I agree, there are many other, perhaps welcome effects, but, in the light of such a serious, long lasting consequence as this, all of those should pale into insignificance.)

Similarly, this system may be prejudicial to upper caste people, but some benefit also is their share. A closer look will show that people of the upper castes, due to, greater opportunities of competition as well as the opportunities for sharper competition that are occurring as a fallout of reservation, are growing further in all faculties at a faster rate.

Considering together both the above effects, the intellectual gap between people of lower caste and those belonging to upper caste will be on the rise as generations go by. A stage will come, certainly in a few generations, making it difficult for the upper and lower caste population to live together in this world, at least as equal beings. The frightening thing is that those of lower caste shall be incapable of realizing their past, that they once were more or less equal to all others. And this might lead to permanent changes in the structure of human race of the future.

This danger can be averted to a great extent if the existing reservation system itself is put to use appropriately. That is to say, the existing system can be re-introduced in a manner befitting, or as an incentive to, growth. For example, 'reservations' can be made available only to jobs needing higher educational or academic qualifications and merit, as a minimum requirement. In which case, those lower in caste shall be forced to attain greater standards of knowledge, skill, and learning. To elaborate, let us say we have introduced a new system of reservation, called 'progressive justice', according to which,

-- All jobs in this country are grouped into different levels; such as level 1 to level 7, with level 1 needing the lowest and level 7 needing the highest entry-level educational status, say level 1 needing a pass in some schooling and level 7 needing the highest qualification with certain research experience.

-- To begin with, reservation is made applicable to all the jobs available, right from level 1 upwards to level 7, at a progressively increasing rate. That is, if 10% of level 1 jobs are reserved for those of lower caste, 12% of level 2 jobs, 15% level of 3 and so on with level 7 showing the maximum say 30%.

-- After some time, say 2 years, the system is subjected to a review when level 1 jobs shall be removed from the domain of reservation. The quantum of reserved positions released can be added to the quota of other higher levels. That is, if 11% level 2 jobs are reserved, 15% level 3 and so on with level 7 showing the maximum, in this case, 35%.

-- After some more time, say another 2 years, the system is again subjected to a review when level 1, as well as level 2 jobs, shall be removed from the ambit of reservation. The quantum of reserved positions thus released can be added to such positions available at other higher levels where it is still in force. That is if 20% level 3 jobs are reserved, 25% level 4 and so on with level 7 showing the maximum say 40%

-- Some more time after that, say another 8 years, when this system of prioritization is subjected to a review there shall be no need to continue this scheme as the ends would have already met.

-- It can be seen that more learned or skilled one is, greater will be the chances of finding a living with ease. Therefore learning, as well as improving one's skill, becomes a necessity. For the present, as those lower in caste can very well earn a living by doing one of the low-paid or menial jobs reserved for them. As a result, learning, acquiring a new skill, or sharpening one's talents are not necessities for them.

As mentioned earlier, the pressing, ardent desire to find an alternative to the 'wild' suggestions of Mahatma Gandhi might have blinded all reformists. Otherwise, nothing can explain their inability to see, at least one such possibility.

In the study focusing on the 'role of education in social mobility within the context of class structure' by Hiroshi Ishida et al, class origin (corresponds to respondent's father's class) and class destination (current class of respondent) are seen to have been influenced by

- Unequal access to education for different class origins. 'Two forms of educational advantage to children of professional and managerial class (read upper castes), a better access to higher levels of education and an avoidance of lower levels'.

- Allocation of class positions (of destination) influenced by class origin. "Here also, wards of highly qualified people have an advantage in access to professional and managerial positions, but they also may be successful in avoiding manual positions. Conversely, wards of poorly qualified are not only excluded from professional and managerial positions, they are more likely to be recruited to manual positions"

Reserving menial and low paid jobs for those low in castes is, needless to say, adding fuel to fire.

Effect of education on class reproduction and mobility is remarkably uniform across nations with the exception of two socialist nations, namely, Poland and Hungary, of the above-mentioned study. In these countries, more people can be seen as choosing manual and unskilled classes as a destination, irrespective of the class origin, which could be attributed to the effect of the prevailing political climate.

In this, a major obstacle to equality of educational opportunity probably comes from the resistance of those of certain class origin (e.g. managerial classes) to low qualifications, in addition to them having better access to high qualifications. While in case of lower classes, even when they were provided with access to high qualifications, as they are now, "the easy availability of low qualifications and the possibility of thus finding a livelihood effectively prevented them from reaching higher destinations". Also, the low classes lack the 'cultural traits' necessary for making one strive hard, or endure pains, to gain entry into higher reaches of the academic world, or dream about climbing the social ladder.

We thus can see, the cultural needs and desires, the fulfillment of which is the yearning of all who try to achieve better positions in life, are not fully developed in the case of lower caste people. And presently, we are doing nothing to inculcate such a desire. Also, we are compounding the situation by making low qualifications sufficient to fetch a living.

Therefore, it is all the more important that this possibility of 'finding a livelihood with low qualifications' is eliminated, if education is to be of use as an expedient. This was clearly noticed while analyzing the dissimilar growth rates in many industrialized nations, which exposed a link between the peoples' desire to excel in life and the actual rate of growth. Also, the desire to do well in life was found to be influenced by many socio-cultural parameters. (see *Hiroshi Ishida, Walter Müller, and John M. Ridge. 1995. "Class Origin, Class Destination, and Education: A Cross-National Study of Ten Industrial Nations". American Journal of Sociology 101: 145-193*)

7.6 Next and probably the ultimate singularity may happen sometime in the future, many (or maybe few) generations from today.

In his well-known essay on Biological Possibilities for the Human Species in the Next Ten Thousand Years, JBS Haldane mentions of the possibility of human species "dividing into two or more branches for development of different human capacities. To me, this is a terrible danger, as such species should fail to understand each other... and such misunderstanding can generate quarrels and even war." (see *http://www.transhumanism.org/resources/Haldanebioposs.htm*)

Another paper on the future of human race mentions that multiculturalism, which is the essence of modern society, is to play a vital role in its future. It shouldn't come as any surprise that humans finally evolve into a single, ubiquitous ethnic group, should the mixing of the cultures continue. As miscegenation becomes commonplace, humans will slowly begin to lose the distinguishing features of their ethnicity, and instead, take on characteristics from many different parts of the world. There's an obvious benefit. All this will reduce "race" to a nonentity, and it will no longer be an issue. One can, however, expect a genetically smart upper class and a dim-witted underclass to emerge.

In still another scenario shown by The Royal Society, normal work itself can be expected to evolve over the next decade. Here, enhancement technologies show great potential to make a very significant contribution. Widespread use of enhancements might influence an individual's ability to learn or perform tasks. This consequently can affect or become part of the profession. Which could influence motivation; or enable people to work in more extreme conditions or into old age, reduce work-related illness; or facilitate earlier return to work after illness. Moreover, this may give rise to the danger of the 'enhanced' population modifying the world in which they live, to their advantage. Consequently, the rest of the people shall get an additional load of accommodating to the changed world. Also, the intellectual gap between different groups of people will be playing a significant part in deciding the path, each culture comes to follow.

(see https://royalsociety.org/policy/projects/humanenhancement /workshop-report/sert)

It should a matter of great concern that the different possibilities of the succession of the humans, though shall be befalling on all cultures, is bound to land an earth-shattering impact on the already stratified and intellectually weakened Indian society. One thing common with all these propositions is the possibility of an inferior group, which shall be at the receiving end of any eventualities. Majority of Indians with their rate of intellectual growth at risk, might find themselves at that end, the 'part, branch or form' of the 'enhanced future species' where no human should be.

Chapter 8

CASTE – A SUMMARY

Caste is a relic of dark ages. In India, it did not evolve into a modernized version in the natural course of events as the people were not the real custodians of their society, having been under foreign rule for many years. And those ruled over this country finding great use in caste, any such prospect would have been brought to an immediate halt.

Other countries had their share of such customs which are even more shocking, like lynching, burning at stake or various entertainments of Roman Empire, all of which, evolved into something more acceptable to society, as time went by. Even in recent times, some nations continued following many questionable practices and one such, in the area of eugenics can be cited as example, where, compulsory abortion or other controls over reproduction is imposed on people.

The medicine which is being tried towards amelioration of the victims of caste is reservation. It can be easily observed that we are applying that cure with no regard to its consequences, just as we followed the caste system with no regard to its ill effects. It is only logical to realize that, even without considering all that is mentioned about its lack of effectiveness, as the cure is not working, we need to change medication

About the Author

He has taken to writing on retirement from Indian Navy in 2013 after a lengthy career, during which he had the good luck to come across as colleagues, subordinates and superiors, a real, wide cross section of India, and quite a few more from the rest of the world. Every second person, during those years, that one had to do business with, thus being from entirely different backgrounds and consequently opening up a kaleidoscopic view of society, he couldn't but reflect on human transactions in many colors, each of them leading to a horde of imponderables, human or non human, living and non living.

Other books by this author

Please visit your favorite ebook retailer to discover other books by Roy T James

The Unsure Male A bold, new, and different look at the enigma of life that explains everything one needs to know.

Hubs that Provoke An oblique view of all that we consider as the most cherished of human values.

Glimpses of Autobiography: A bunch of people, their impressions, and thoughts that would have found a place in his autobiography, had he wrote one

More hubs that Provoke: Some more, about all that we consider as the most cherished values in life

Homo-posterus: A science fiction novel

Easy Route to Peace: A collection of essays proposing a few quick and easy ways to simplify the complex life, we have made for ourselves.

Life of Style: A peep into the human society to see why it is always into violence.

Overhaul Life: Isn't there a need to overhaul life?